Elizabeth Ma'am was a teacher like none other but ...

our teacher

Sundara Ramaswamy

Art by Neeta Gangopadhyay

KATHA

Translated from the Tamil by
Malati Mathur

Chapter 1

The Maharajas who lived all those years ago must have loved Saraswati, the Goddess of Learning. Why else did they raise such an awesome building. Jaws drop when people are told that this is a high school. Visitors from nearby towns murmur that not even college buildings match its grandeur. I was in class eight then. For the second time. That was the year I began to fail. That was also the year that Elizabeth Thomas joined our school. For months we had heard, she's coming, she's coming, she's coming. Finally, she did!

Padmavathi Ma'am was the only woman teacher in our school of forty teachers. And she often complained bitterly about this, or so our Section B friends said. She was fed up. Completely! She was just waiting for the Inspector of Schools to visit, so she could tell him so herself.

"I am sure she will soon resign, our Padmavathi Ma'am," Seshan said matter-of-factly one day. Seshan had a great imagination, matched only by his height. Let a fight break out, and out would come his deadly sharpened pencil. Jab, Jab, Jab! Oh yes, he and his pencil were famous in the whole school.

Chapter 2

Padmavathi Ma'am did complain to the Inspector when he made his annual visit. And her prayers were answered.

Elizabeth Thomas arrived. All the way from north Travancore.

Every single student was there in front of the Assembly Hall to catch the first glimpse of the new teacher. The girls stood expectantly peering from one side of the wide staircase, clutching the railing, jostling one another, ripples of laughter spreading up and down the stairs.

Padmavathi Ma'am descended the stairs, her left hand delicately holding up the pleats of her chocolate brown silk sari. She walked over to Elizabeth Thomas with a smile, took her hands in a warm clasp and led her into the Visitors' Room, as one would a child.

That was all. But that moment is still very clearly imprinted in my memory.

One little girl nudged her friend, "Who do you think is prettier, di?"

She did not notice the Headmaster standing right behind her. Raising his hands, he thundered, "What's going on here!" The girls gathered their skirts and fled.

But we all asked the same question too.

But the answer always changed depending on the day, time and angle from which we saw them.

But we all definitely saw that Padmavathi Ma'am's make-up gradually became gaudier.

Both women were almost the same age. Together they would sway in, in the gentle glow of morning, decked up in flowers, smiles and soft words. It took them a long time to reach the school building from the gate at the far end of the compound wall. As they came nearer, they would try to stretch out the minutes and pause every few yards to chat. We would watch, fascinated, until the sloping roof of the verandah hid their feet.

A few seconds later, the appearance of a pair of dark heads adorned with flowers, above the stairs of the examination hall, invariably gave us a stab of pleasure.

We talked and dreamt of them constantly. This was not just because they loved us or taught us well. It was the friendship they shared. The intimacy that had blossomed between them found an echo in ours. We loved to talk about how much they loved each other.

Chapter 3

If only this beautiful song of friendship had played on without any jarring notes.

But then things don't always happen the way we wish them to.

Section B was doing so much better than us that even the tallest of ladders couldn't have helped us reach the marks they scored in exams.

No, they weren't all geniuses. But they had Padmavathi Ma'am. She could drill facts into the thickest of heads, as if she opened up each skull and stuffed it with knowledge.

Everyone knew and acknowledged this fact.

Last year, when he was giving away the Seethalakshmi Annual Memorial Prize for Excellence, even our Headmaster had praised her.

“If Madam Padmavathi sets her mind to it, even a mouse would know the Pythagoras Theorem inside out!” he had proudly said.

This was almost true. Her student, B Raman, had again walked off with cent percent marks in maths in the quarterly exams that year. Our own genius, Specs Sarojini had barely scraped in seventy.

Most in our class, including me, had failed miserably.

All zeroes!

Chapter 4

So when Elizabeth Ma'am arrived, we happily delivered ourselves into her hands.

Day 1, she walked up and down the aisle between our desks asking us to call out our quarterly marks.

We muttered the numbers.

But she didn't even wrinkle her pretty forehead. She just wrote out a simple sum on the blackboard. "Easy, isn't it?" she said with a smile.

But even that easy sum was too much for most of us. Some of us knew the steps, but could not reach the answer. Soon she discovered most of us couldn't even do class 7 sums. Shame on us!

But she just laughed. "Did you crawl into this class from class 7?" she asked.

We smiled back sheepishly.

"Never mind. I promise you will all march into class 9 like smart young soldiers!" She was silent a long while. Then added, "Of course, I will need your help too."

We all nodded our heads vigorously.

She had won us over on the very first day!

From that day on she began to teach us from scratch. She explained the same lesson over and over again. She gave us weekly tests. Homework. And she corrected everything we did, every day. As if punishing herself for all the sins of all our previous teachers.

We felt sorry for her. We all started studying hard, each one of us, so she would not be disappointed. And besides, she was such a whizz. She made maths so exciting that for the first time, the numbers truly came alive for us.

Chapter 5

One day, she casually said, "We are going to get the Seethalakshmi Annual Memorial Prize this year."

It was a bombshell. What!? One of us could score a whole hundred in Maths in the final exams?

We sat in complete silence.

"What's the matter? Has no one anything to say? You, Sarojini?"

Sarojini bowed her head, her earrings swinging.

"We will win the Prize," Elizabeth Ma'am repeated firmly.

A thrill ran down our backs. How could her words not come true? Is there anything she could not help us achieve?

As the days went by, we too started believing that we would truly win the prize.

We started
walking past
Section B with
heads held high.
This even led to a fight once.

One morning, I and my
friends were loitering in the
corridor outside our classroom
when Seshan and his gang, and
B Raman and his pals joined us.
Enemies from Section B.

And guess what that fool of a Kitta does?
"We are going to grab the Seethalakshmi Annual
Memorial Prize this year!" he blurts out.

That was it! Seshan was instantly on the warpath.

"Who says so?"

"Our ma'am, that's who."

"Oh, so your ma'am can predict the future, can she?"

My friend Kolappan elbowed his way to the front. "She can't, but she can teach well."

Kolappan was one of the August revolutionaries. He had joined the movement to drive the British out from our country. He had even spent a night in prison. Anyone opposing him would have been promptly boycotted by the entire student community.

“There is not one fellow in India who can outshine B Raman in Maths,” Seshan stubbornly persisted.

“Useless Raman!” screeched Shamu. “Saapatu Raman, greedy Raman.”

“I’ll knock your teeth out,” growled Seshan.

“Go ahead, try!” said Shamu, helpfully thrusting his nose into Seshan’s glowering face.

Seshan grabbed him and thrust him violently away even as he raised a victory cheer, "Padmavathi Ma'am, Jai!"

"Jai! Jai! Jai!" sang out his gang.

Why would we stay quiet? We stood up for our own teacher, shouting, "Jai! Jai! Elizabeth Ma'am, Jai!" And for good measure, added, "Jai! Mahatma Gandhi, Jai!"

Seshan pulled his famous pencil out of his pocket and started sharpening it menacingly.

Fortunately, the bell rang just then and we hurried into our classrooms.

Our Ma'am heard what happened. She scolded us. It seems Padmavathi Ma'am had complained that we had made fun of her.

Kolappan stood up. "They say we cannot win the Prize," he declared loudly. Then muttered, "My blood boils."

Chapter 6

Elizabeth Ma'am's confidence and our hard work was not wasted. We all did well and raked in the marks at the half-yearly examinations. And Specs Sarojini scored a full hundred in Maths! She had planted our flag high on Mount Everest! The papers had been corrected by Padmavathi Ma'am, the marks awarded in her own hand on each paper.

I don't remember what that Maths King, B Raman, scored. But I do remember that it wasn't hundred. Because the whole of Section B grumbled that our teacher had set a very difficult paper.

"You need brains to solve Elizabeth Ma'am's paper, you asses," taunted Kolappan.

Another fight was brewing.

"Meet outside school, then we'll see," growled Seshan.

"Hah, you mosquito! We are so VERY scared of you!" smirked Kolappan.

Section B was on the warpath now.

Our Headmaster came to our class the day the answer books were distributed and lavished praise on our teacher.

Elizabeth Ma'am blushed red and lowered her eyes to the floor. We respectfully rose when he left the room, but Ma'am even forgot to tell us to sit down again.

She looked proudly at each one of us. Then she started laughing. Slowly, the soft chuckle turned into happy, uncontrolled laughter.

And we all laughed with her.

“You are shining examples, each one of you,” she said. Walking up to Sarojini, she patted her back fondly.

Specs Sarojini stood up then and said something that we couldn’t hear.

But Ma’am’s expression changed abruptly and she sat down clumsily in her chair. We could see she was struggling not to cry in front of us.

“Ma’am, what is it, Ma’am?”

The bell rang just then.

Elizabeth Ma’am stood up. “Sarojini, did the girl say that Padmavathi Ma’am actually said this herself?”

“Yes Ma’am.”

Her eyes brimmed over as she stared at the wall, avoiding our eyes.

"Did I tell any of you the questions?" she asked us, her voice quivering.

We couldn't quite understand what she meant. We sat there gaping at each other, not knowing what to say.

"Did I tell you anything?" she asked once more. The question dissolved into silence, breaking our hearts.

"God knows the truth," she said softly and left the room.

Chapter 7

How could Padmavathi Ma'am be so heartless! Elizabeth Thomas would never have told us what questions she had set for the exam. In fact, we hadn't known until then that she had set the question paper. I don't even remember her giving us similar questions to solve in our practice sessions.

This was a plain and outrageous lie!

If Elizabeth Ma'am grew cactii, each thorny plant would have burst with fragrant blossoms. She could turn sand into gold. Why, the whole school knew that everyone who'd come to teach us earlier had thrown up their hands in despair before us. But not Elizabeth Thomas.

She had asked us to hold up our heads in pride and self-confidence. And work hard. We had only done what she asked us to do. And we had done well!

Jealousy, it was pure jealousy.

No, Ma'am, we all rushed to tell her. You told us nothing.

Elizabeth Ma'am did not come to school the next day.

Suddenly a rumour spread that she would never come back.

So now, what would happen to us? Tossed around from teacher to teacher. Was this to be our fate?

But Elizabeth Ma'am walked in the next day just as the bell rang, almost as if she could not resist the sound of the bell. She showed no signs of sadness as she taught with her usual enthusiasm.

But from that day on, we never saw her and Padmavathi Ma'am together again. Ever.

Then the final exams approached. Elizabeth Ma'am said without the slightest hesitation, "My class will win the Seethalakshmi Annual Memorial Prize this time."

"This time the prize will definitely be ours, Ma'am," said Kitta.

"You also feel that way? Excellent!" she said happily.

Then looking down at her fingernails, she said in a very quiet voice, "But the question papers are being set in another city. So I won't be able to tell you the questions as I had done earlier." And she smiled a sad, desolate smile.

So that sharp thorn was still lodged inside her.

We were all determined to win the prize. It would declare her innocence loud and clear. And also establish how smart Section A was.

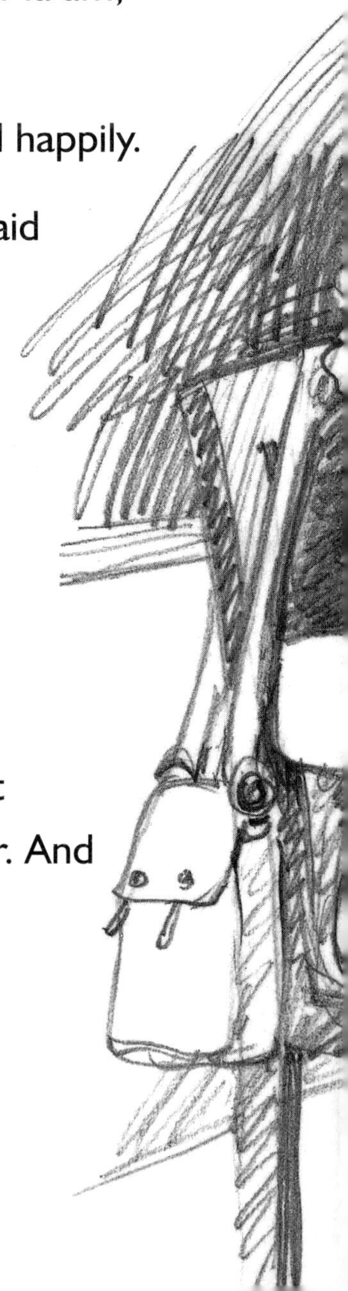

When the Headmaster placed the
prize in her hands, the applause
would pierce the one who had
spread such lies and slander!
We had to win the prize.

Chapter 8

The exams were now upon us. But Elizabeth Ma'am made us feel as if we were off to wage a battle, and the whole nation depended only on our courage.

We worked hard. We studied, revised, brushed up each and every problem, helped one another with questions and doubts. Even on Saturdays. And she was with us all the way, never taking a minute off.

We had to win the prize if only to put it into her hands. She truly deserved it.

The final exam seemed to be a test for her rather than us.

It was the last day. The Maths exam was on when it happened.

Five minutes were left before the final bell.

Sarojini stood up to hand in her answer paper.

Elizabeth Ma'am came up to her and softly said, "You still have time. Why don't you check your paper again?"

Her voice reached me, a few desks away. Sensing a difference in her tone, I looked up.

Sarojini sat down obediently and started to turn the pages reluctantly.

The final bell sounded. Elizabeth Ma'am quickly walked over to her and said, "Have you reviewed all your answers right upto the last sum?" Then she walked away briskly, collecting answer books.

Sarojini sat down hastily, turned to the last page, and made some corrections.

"I strongly object to your action!" roared a voice.

It was Padmavathi Ma'am. Her voice echoed sharply through the examination hall.

Followed by the clattering of her chappals as she went up the stairs.

The enquiry began.

At first, Elizabeth Ma'am refused to answer any of the questions the Headmaster asked her, standing still and lifeless as a statue.

"This is my last question," the Headmaster finally said. "When you asked Sarojini to go over her work again, were you indicating to her indirectly that she should correct a wrong answer?"

There was a long silence. Then our teacher said, "I was."

The Headmaster went upstairs. By the time I came out, she had reached the far end of the verandah. I could see her moving like a shadow against the wall.

If a dream is shattered, the disappointment can be borne. But this was different – it was humiliating for her to even stand in front of us, her head bowed in shame. Even after twenty years, I am overcome by sadness whenever I think of it.

I never saw Elizabeth
Ma'am again after that day.